THE BEST OF
Shania Twain

ISBN 0-634-00472-7

HAL•LEONARD®
CORPORATION
7777 W. BLUEMOUND RD. P.O. BOX 13819 MILWAUKEE, WI 53213

Visit Hal Leonard Online at
www.halleonard.com

THE BEST OF
Shania Twain

Contents

Any Man of Mine

Words and Music by SHANIA TWAIN
and R.J. LANGE

(Drums & handclaps)

(Spoken:)   *"This is what a woman wants..."*

An - y man of mine bet - ter be proud of ____ me. E - ven when I'm ug - ly, he

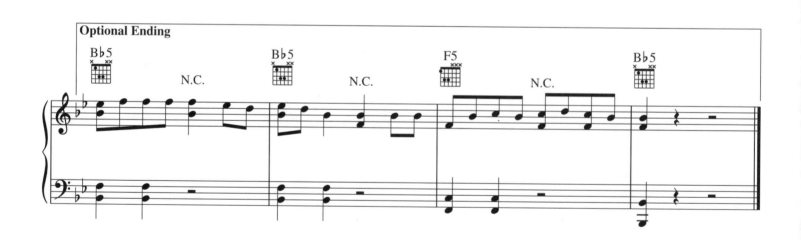

Additional Lyrics

(Spoken:) You gotta shimmy, shake, make the earth quake.
Kick, turn, stomp, stomp, then you jump heel to toe. Do-si-do
'Til your boots wanna break, 'til your feet and your back ache.
Keep it movin' 'til you just can't take anymore.
Come on, everybody on the floor, a-one two, a-three four.
Hup two, hup if you wanna be a man of mine, that's right.
This is what a woman wants...

Don't Be Stupid
(You Know I Love You)

Words and Music by SHANIA TWAIN
and R.J. LANGE

Come On Over

Words and Music by SHANIA TWAIN
and R.J. LANGE

Moderate Calypso Rock

Get a life, _

D.S. al Coda

Get a life,

CODA

load off your mind, __ yeah. Come on o-

-ver, __ come on in. _____ Yeah, come on, come _ on.

From This Moment On

Words and Music by SHANIA TWAIN
and R.J. LANGE

* Male vocals sung an octave higher throughout.

Home Ain't Where His Heart Is Anymore

Words and Music by SHANIA TWAIN
and R.J. LANGE

knew _ how _ to reach _ me deep _ in - side, _ and he found a part _ of me _ I could not hide. And we'd walk and talk _ and touch _ ten - der - ly, _

He

* Melody is written an octave higher than sung.

Honey, I'm Home

Words and Music by SHANIA TWAIN
and R.J. LANGE

Moderate Country Rock

The car won't start, it's

fall-ing a-part.__ I was late for work__ and the boss got smart. My

(If You're Not In It for Love)
I'm Outta Here!

Words and Music by SHANIA TWAIN
and R.J. LANGE

Love Gets Me Every Time

Words and Music by SHANIA TWAIN
and R.J. LANGE

The Woman in Me
(Needs the Man in You)

Words and Music by SHANIA TWAIN
and R.J. LANGE

Slowly

I'm not al - ways

strong,

and some - times ___ I'm e - ven wrong.

But I win when ___ I choose, and I can't stand ___ to lose. But I can't al - ways

No One Needs to Know

Words and Music by SHANIA TWAIN
and R.J. LANGE

-ly, on - ly he ___ can make ___ it right. ___

Instrumental solo

Solo ends And I'm not lone -

That Don't Impress Me Much

Words and Music by SHANIA TWAIN
and R.J. LANGE

Whose Bed Have Your Boots Been Under?

Words and Music by SHANIA TWAIN
and R.J. LANGE

Whose bed have your boots been un-der? __

Whose bed have your boots been un - der? __

And whose heart did you steal, I won - der? __ This time __ did it

Solo ends   (Sung:) So ___

___   next   time   you're

CODA

feel   like   thun - der?

D.S. al Coda

N.C.

Whose   bed   have   your   boots   been   un - der? ___   And   whose   heart   did   you

You're Still the One

Words and Music by SHANIA TWAIN
and R.J. LANGE

You Win My Love

Words and Music by
R.J. LANGE

Moderately fast Rock

mf

I'm look-in' for a lov-er who can rev his lit-tle en - gine up.

He can have a fif-ty-five Chev-y or a fan-cy lit-tle pick-up truck.